iCEBREAKERS

At last . . . 303 ways to really "BREAK THE ICE" in your cell group!

Edited by
Randall G. Neighbour

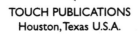

TOUCH PUBLICATIONS
Houston, Texas U.S.A.

Published by TOUCH Publications
P.O. Box 19888
Houston, Texas 77224-9888 U.S.A.
(281) 497-7901 • Fax (281) 497-0904

Cover design by Don Bleyl
Text design by Rick Chandler

ISBN: 1-880828-14-6

TOUCH Publications is the book-publishing
division of TOUCH Outreach Ministries, a
resource and consulting ministry for churches
with a vision for cell-based local church
structure.

Find us on the World Wide Web at
http://www.touchusa.org

Acknowledgments

*Special thanks to all
of the cell leaders and
cell members who contributed
their best icebreakers!*

Rich Bersett
Brian Bungee
Doug Carr
John Daye
Dave Fiksen
B. J. Fink
Rebecca Forehand
Krista Griffin
Anna Hambly
James Hoefer
Jackie Howard

Jim Huth
Bonnie Kahn
Clark Killingsworth
Richard Kuebler
Randy Pruett
Robert and Cindy Read
Phil Shand
Samuel Shreffler
Paul Smith
Branan Ward
Sung-Hee Yun

Contents

Introduction

Icebreakers Are Fun!

Years ago, my wife and I led a cell group of young professionals. These young adults had good jobs, were serious about their walk with God and gave themselves to the group in a special way. Each week we gathered to worship, share, eat, laugh and be transparent about tough issues in our lives.

About three months into cell life, we had one meeting I'll never forget. The icebreaker question was, "If you could change one thing about your person, what would it be?" One by one, each person shared. One young woman said she didn't like her blonde hair because people thought she was all looks and no brains.

I said I'd like to lose weight. The next person said he wanted a smaller nose. Then Lee raised his right elbow and said, "I want to raise my right arm above my head."

The room went silent. There we were, bringing up trivial things when this dear guy had a real physical handicap! I sensed from the look of shock on everyone's faces that I needed to say something fast. I turned to him and asked, "Lee, would you like us to pray with you for healing for your shoulder?" Lee replied, "Naw. I just want to raise my arm above my head and pull a cold soda out of my armpit any time I am thirsty."

That night we learned that Lee had a twisted sense of humor and trusted us enough to share it. Through the months, we bonded as a team and reached out to unbelievers. Some of my deepest friendships were formed in that group. Now I won't be so bold as to claim our group was great because of some wacky icebreakers, but I will say that we never would have teamed up so well for ministry if we hadn't had them to open our meetings.

This booklet is filled with questions that you can use to open your group meetings. Group leaders just like you sent them to me, and I think it's a great collection. Take a few minutes to read the following paragraphs before you launch into the book. The information is helpful and will guide you to choose the question best suited for your group members and for the group's level of maturity.

What Is an Icebreaker?

An icebreaker is a simple question that helps people feel comfortable in a group setting. An icebreaker helps individuals focus on others. This sets a good tone for a small group or cell group meeting.

Why Use an Icebreaker?

Icebreakers are vital to the growth of a small group or cell group. People don't quickly divulge needs and hurts in a group setting. They have to practice sharing and learn that it's safe to share deep things. Without icebreakers, your group won't have the freedom to share openly about difficult issues. Consider an icebreaker as the first step in preparation for swimming. If you don't learn simple breathing techniques, you'll be frightened and drown! Small group gatherings are no different. If you want your group to dive into deep issues, the regular use of an icebreaker will be a great "big toe in the water."

Icebreakers also help you learn things about your cell members that you might never discover otherwise. At the start of one meeting, the cell leader asked, "What was your favorite toy as a child?" Most shared about toys like G.I. Joe or a special doll. One woman said, "I grew up in Germany during World War II and at that time I did not have a toy. I lived with my sister in an underground tunnel." As the group began expressing sympathy for her plight, she said, "I didn't need a toy. I had my sister." It would have taken months for this shy woman to share this way. Yet, with this simple question, the group saw a new side of her life.

How Long Should Icebreakers Take?

The typical icebreaker takes a minute or less for each person to answer. Some can take longer, but watch your time! You'll invest an entire hour of your meeting if every person in a group of 12 shares for five minutes.

Different Types of Icebreakers

There are thousands of questions you can ask a group of people, but only a few will achieve the right goals for your group. When your group is new, choose icebreakers that will introduce the history of each member (brothers and sisters, the kind of car the family had while growing up, etc.) and questions that will help everyone feel at ease ("If you were a cucumber, what kind of pickle would you want to be when you grew up?"). The deciding factor is the depth of the relationships in the room. If you've been together for a few months, a serious question such as, "What's the biggest thing that happened to you last week?" is quite appropriate.

Icebreakers for Stages of Cell Life

There are five stages of cell life: acquaintance, conflict, community, outreach and multiplication. Each stage requires a different kind of question. The longer a group is together, the deeper the questions can go. But don't forget that the icebreaker is a question to focus everyone on the time together, not a launch into ministry time (see "Bad Icebreakers" below for more information).

How to Facilitate a Good Icebreaker

The best way to facilitate the icebreaker is to share the question and then answer it yourself within the time limit. Then turn to the person on your right or your left and ask him or her to share. This does two things: models the time limit and gives a good example of an answer. Most folks catch on after one or two responses and don't have to ask for clarification.

Always move around the circle person by person, and ask everyone to hold additional comments until after the meeting. This tells talkers that they can answer the icebreaker only one time. It also gives quiet people permission to share so that they are not the last folks to answer the question every week.

Give people permission to "pass" so they won't feel as though they're being put on the spot. Some people need more "prep" or "thinking" time than others. Then, when everyone else has answered, ask those who passed whether they'd like to answer. Most will.

The icebreaker is also one of the best parts of the meeting to delegate to a group member. It's easy to share this part of the meeting. Inviting others to lead part of the meeting creates ownership among group members.

How to Handle the Unexpected During an Icebreaker

What do you do when someone blurts out something really heavy during the icebreaker? ("I lost my job." "My father died yesterday." "My wife walked out on me.") Thank the person for sharing such a deep need right away. Then say that you'd like to pray for him or her just after a time of worship, when the cell members are able to minister better. This way you won't enter a ministry time before preparing your heart, and the entire meeting (and maybe subsequent meetings) won't focus on just one person.

What if someone shares something inappropriate about a spouse, parent or church member during the icebreaker? These are very embarrassing moments! Tell the person that this might not be the best time or place to share this kind of issue. Then turn to the whole group and say, "This group is a safe place. Here you are loved and no word or action can make us dislike you." Display unconditional love. Then move on as quickly as you are able. There's nothing more embarrassing than dwelling on it!

Occasionally a simple question can hit on deep hurts and needs. I was leading a group a few years ago and asked a basic question: "How many brothers and sisters do you have, and where did you grow up as a kid?" We went around the room and by the time the third person shared, a woman whose sister had died rushed out of the room crying. Although her sister had passed away a year before and she seemed to be coping well, she was still privately grieving. While the question was innocent enough, the cell member was hurt that I would ask it knowing about her loss. I felt horrible. Even though I apologized, mending that relationship took weeks. Truth is, I came up with the question during refreshment time just before we began. Had I prayed about the icebreaker and prepared, I would have chosen another question.

Make sure you pray carefully about the questions you pose to your group. If you find yourself on the way to your group meeting without an icebreaker, bounce the question off your spouse or intern and ask if the group would feel comfortable with the question. He or she may be thinking about people's feelings when you are not, or may know or sense something that you have not noticed.

Take Time to Train Others!

When you're teaching others how to do this part of the meeting (and you should be), ask them to watch you and give you feedback after the meeting. Then, give one of them the icebreaker the following week and visit afterward about how it was handled and what needs improvement. After a couple of times, they will tell you what they would have done better or how great it went. It's not hard to give away the icebreaker if you model the right way. It's on-the-job training, and it's the easiest part of a meeting to delegate to an emerging leader, a child, a quiet spouse or a newcomer.

Bad Icebreakers

One young leader of a cell was as serious as a heart attack most of the time. He was highly self-disciplined and very devoted to the Lord. As the intern, he was asked to share an icebreaker. He asked, "What is one thing that made you angry this week?" He answered his own question by telling the group that he was upset with the cell leader. The rest of the group followed suit and began to relentlessly critique the cell leader.

Bad icebreakers invite people to reveal the hurts and sins of others in the room or are inappropriate or too personal for a group setting. If you lead off your group meeting with a question that is inappropriate ("Share the thing you hate the most about the person on your left") or "too close for comfort," your members won't answer truthfully or they'll "pass!" If you're not sure whether the question is appropriate, ask. Share the question and then ask the group whether they want to answer it. If anyone rejects it, ask a better question. The last thing you want to do is alienate your group members in the first five minutes of your meeting. See page 145 for some more examples of bad icebreakers.

It's Your Turn
That's enough training. You're probably itching to get to the questions, so dive in and find the right one! Some of the best times in my life have

occurred in cell meetings. I have laughed so hard that I got sick to my stomach. I've cried so hard with other members that I thought I was going to need a bucket to catch the tears. I'll never forget the time I visited a cell group at another church and the icebreaker was, "What kind of music do you listen to in your car?" We went around the room and one guy said, "I don't listen to music in the car. I listen to my wife tell me what's wrong with my driving."

Remember that there are no bad answers to the questions in this book. But if you don't ask an icebreaker question, you might be in for a bad meeting! Icebreakers are revealing and a lot of fun. Intimacy in a small group setting begins with a handshake or an icebreaker.

Catch-Up

What was the most significant thing
that happened to you last week?

How did God bless you
last week?

How would you describe your
week in terms of a car (sports car,
clunker, luxury sedan, etc.)?

What was the best thing about your week?

If you could share one thing that happened since we last met, what would it be?

Light-Hearted
and Welcoming

What is the most fulfilling work
you have ever done?

What is your worst haircut/
hairdo story? (2-minute time limit)

What's the best gift you received
as a child?

Share one of your strengths.

Who was your favorite
childhood friend? Why?

What is your favorite insect?

∀

Complete the following:
"People might be surprised to
find out that I _____."

∀

What would you do if you could
take a day off work this week?

∀

What's your favorite scar on your
body? How did you get it?

❥

Which rooms in your house do
you like best?

❥

What is the most expensive gift
someone has given you?

❥

As a child, who was your
favorite babysitter?

Name a vehicle that best describes
you and explain why.

Describe yourself using a symbol
(A pen and paper will be needed).

Does your name have a special
meaning? Were you named after
someone special?

Which of the following restrictions
could you best tolerate:
leaving the country permanently,
or never leaving the state in
which you now live?

When was the last time you did
something for the first time?

∀

Which of your clothes are your favorites?

∀

Describe your week by using a car engine analogy (i.e. overheated, cruising, idle, etc.).

∀

What is the best compliment you have ever received?

❯

Who was your hero when you were
growing up? How did you try to
imitate him or her?

❯

Who was the most interesting person
who ever visited you or your family?

❯

What is one thing you like
about your life?

If someone were to ask you a
question guaranteed to get you
talking, what would that question be?

What was the first trip you
remember taking with your family
and what do you most remember
about it?

What was your first nickname?

If you could take a pill that would enable you to live until you reach 1,000 years old, would you do it? Why or why not?

Which actor or actress would best play you?

▼

What is your favorite hobby
or sport, and how did you
get started?

▼

What are three of your favorite
activities?

▼

When you are cold, where do
you like to get warm?

❯

Whom do you respect the most?

❯

Describe your week in colors.

❯

Have you ever wanted to trade lives
with another person?
With whom?

What was your funniest dream?

What's your favorite kind of pillow
(feather, flat, body or throw)?

What's your favorite store?
Which is your favorite aisle?

What's your favorite seat in an airplane (front, back, window, aisle, middle)?

When and how did you learn to drive an automobile?

What animal best describes your personality?

∀

Have you ever had a favorite
outfit (clothes) that others
thought was ugly?

∀

What's the longest phone
conversation you have ever had and
with whom were you speaking?

∀

Which shoe do you put on first?

❦

What ability do you possess that
you like the most?

❦

Who is your favorite detective
of all time?

❦

Describe your favorite family pet
from anytime in your life.

❖

What's the best thing that happened
to you during the last year?

❖

Do you exercise regularly?
Why or why not?

Do you put the grocery cart back
when you go to the supermarket?
Why or why not?

❖

I am most like my Dad in
that I _____?

❖

I am most like my Mom in
that I _____?

❖

What is your favorite
junk food?

∇

Who was your first friend and how
long were you friends?

∇

Share one affirming thing about
the person to your right.

∇

When you were sick as a child,
how did your parents make
you feel better?

❖

What would be your ideal vacation?

❖

What is your favorite comic strip?

❖

What is your favorite television
show?

What is your favorite book?

What kind of music do you listen to
in the car?

What's the best thing for you to
do when you feel yourself
becoming angry?

What is your favorite time of day
and why?

Using a fruit or vegetable, describe
your life this week (dried fig, ripe
cantaloupe, smashed banana, hot
jalapeno, sour grapes, etc.).

What does your dream car look like?

❤

Name three activities you like to do
with your friends.

❤

Describe your "perfect"
evening out.

❤

If your electricity went out for
a week, what would you miss
the most?

⩔

What is your most treasured
memory?

⩔

Complete the following: "Just for fun,
before I die I'd like to _____."

⩔

Which animal best describes your
mood right now?

How much did you pay for the
shoes you are wearing?

Name your favorite U.S. President.
Why is he your favorite?

Tell us about the first toy you
remember.

What was the first family car you
remember? What do you still
remember about it?

What is the best advice you have
ever received?

What is the best meal you've
ever eaten?

What is the worst meal
you've ever eaten?

What is the best trip you have
ever taken?

What is the worst trip you have
ever taken?

∀

What is the dumbest thing you
ever spent money on?

∀

What is the most adventurous
thing you ever did?

∀

What is the nicest thing anybody
has ever said to you?

What is the oldest piece of clothing
that you still wear?

What is the smallest amount
of money you made per hour
on any job?

What is your favorite Christmas tree
ornament?

What is your favorite recreation?

On what popular magazine
cover would your face most
likely appear?

What was the favorite Christmas
present you gave someone?

What was the worst decision you
ever made with a vehicle?

Name your favorite vacation
destination.

Describe your first date.

ϒ

What is the silliest pet name you
ever heard and what was the pet?

ϒ

What do you or did you call your
grandparents and why?

ϒ

What do you have a lot of
in your home?

What do you think you will be
like in 10 years?

When you were little, what did
you want to be
"when you grew up"?

As a child, what did you call your pet
and why?

Use weather terminology to
describe your past week.

Going Deeper

If you could tell your boss anything,
what would it be?

Describe a time when either you lied
to someone or someone lied to you.
How did it make you feel?

What's the worst storm or disaster
you've ever been in?

❖

What did you not like about yourself
as a teen that you have changed?

❖

What person has impacted your life
the most (cannot be God or the
person who led you to Christ)?

What is the last totally unselfish
thing you did?

❯

What is the toughest holiday you
ever faced as a child and why?

❯

What is your greatest need for the
coming year?

❯

What one smell provokes the
strongest memories?

∀

What was the worst career mistake
you ever made?

∀

What is the longest time you went
without sleep? Why?

∀

When somebody tells you that you
are doing something wrong, what's
your reaction?

❖

Would you move to a distant country
for someone you love even if it means
there is very little chance of seeing
your family and friends again?

What is your most compulsive habit?
How do you try to break it?

Where do you feel most trapped?

What one thing would you change
about the way you were raised?

What topic, if any, is too serious
to be joked about?

❖

What do you want to be
remembered for?

❯

Which of your birthdays brings back
the most memories, and why?

❯

Whom have you recently tried to
please and why?

❯

You lend your best friend an
item and it's returned damaged.
What do you do?

❧

You're in a store and you
see a mother hitting a child in
an abusive way. You:

  a. Tell her to stop.
  b. Call the police.
  c. Pray.

❧

After a busy day, how do
you unwind?

Share an opportunity you had this
week to become "stressed out"
and how you dealt with it.

Tell us one thing you have learned
about yourself this year.

If you could change anything from
your past, what would it be?

If you could get one thing through
your child's or parent's head,
what would it be?

If you could give one piece of advice,
what would it be?

What did you learn this week?

❯

You discover your wonderful
one-year-old child is not yours due
to a mix-up at the hospital.
Would you exchange the child
to try to correct the mistake?

❯

Did you like high school? Why or
why not? What would you do
differently?

v

A friend is not taking care of his
or her looks. Do you say so?

v

Do you like to go to parties?
Why or why not?

v

How long have you ever held a
grudge against someone?
How did you resolve it?

Did your parents spank you or put you in "time out"?

Do you have a closer relationship with your mother or with your father? Why?

Do you express your feelings verbally? Why or why not?

What do you do with gifts you
don't like?

When was the last time you told
someone, "I love you"? Do you say
"I love you" easily?

Do you still ask your parents for
help when you get into trouble?

❯

Are you uncomfortable going to
dinner or a movie alone?
How about on vacation?

❯

Do you usually do what *you* want to
do or what *somebody else* likes to do?

❯

Have you ever been caught telling
a lie? What happened?

◂

How do you feel about old people?
What is "old" to you?

◂

How do you think people
describe you?

◂

Name one "old way" you've tried to
get rid of.

How much do you laugh during
the week?

If someone killed a family member,
would you forgive him or her?

You find out that your best friend
is a practicing homosexual.
What do you do?

If you asked your family members
what you complain about most, what
would they say? Why do you
complain about that?

Would you give up 75% of what you
own for a pill that would
permanently change you so
that one hour of sleep
each day would fully refresh you?
Why?

▽

Do you want to be rich?
Why or why not?

▽

For what in your life do you feel
most grateful?

▽

Where do you go or
what do you do when life gets
stressful?

V

How do you react when someone
gives you a compliment?

V

What do you like most about your
life? The least?

V

When was the last time you stole
something?

❖

Would you prefer to be blind
or deaf?

❖

What is your greatest joy?
Sorrow? Challenge?

When did you last cry in front
of another person?
By yourself?

What is the hardest thing you have
ever had to tell somebody?

What are holidays like
with your family?

❖

What do you respect the most
about your parents?

When you disagree with somebody, do you isolate or fight it out?

Using the game of football as an analogy of life, where would you place yourself: outside the park, in the grandstand or on the field?

◥

Share about the most important
day of your life.

◥

If your friends and family were
willing to tell you what they thought
of you, would you want them to?
Why or why not?

A Look at the
Spiritual Side of Life

What person would you love to
see accept Christ as Savior and
Lord this week?

How do you explain the gifts of the
Holy Spirit to somebody who does
not believe in them?

How do you deal with a bad
situation?

When did you last feel the joy of serving someone?

Where were you when you last prayed deeply? Did the environment help or hinder your praying?

What is the best thing about our church?

❤

What do you like most about
our pastor?

❤

Do you take a Sabbath rest
every week?

❤

Do you tell people about your past
sins? Why or why not?

❯

How has God used you recently?

❯

What is the most meaningful thing you have done for someone else?

❯

Have you ever shared a deep struggle with a close friend? How did it make you feel?

If you could ask Noah one question,
what would it be?

When did you sense God's
presence this week?

In what specific way have you grown
in Christ this past month?

If you could pray one person to
Christ this month, how much time
would you dedicate to it?

If you could see one celebrity get
saved, who would it be?

If you were to die tonight, would you
be right with God?

▼

How do you feel about tithing?

▼

What does the word "hate"
mean to you?

▼

What is your spiritual temperature
tonight (use the degrees on a
thermometer to describe where
you are)? Why?

∀

Tell us one thing you have learned
about God this year.

∀

What part of your personality is
God changing right now?

∀

If you could ask Jesus to change
one thing in the world today,
what would it be?

What are you currently trusting God
for that only He can do?

What does heaven look
like to you?

When the Group Multiplies

How do you feel about multiplying?

What have you learned during
this cell cycle?

What is one thing that the Lord
did for you through someone
else in this cell?

What was the hardest thing you
learned during this cell cycle?

Give one word to describe the
group's time together.

Does anything scare you about
multiplying? What?

∀

What gives you joy about
multiplying?

∀

Have you experienced multiplication
before? How is this the same
or different?

∀

What was the hardest stage
in this cell?

Y

What was the easiest stage in this cell?

Y

What are you going to do differently in your next cell group?

Y

What did you learn from one of your cell members during this cycle?

What did you learn from your cell
leader that impacted you the most?

What act of service changed your
life during this cycle?

Recall one moment in cell life that
made a big impact on your life.

What did you learn about reaching
out to the lost during this cell cycle?

What prayers were answered for
you during this cell cycle?

Did you bring anybody to visit during
this cell cycle? Who do you want to
invite to the next cell group?

▼

How long did it take the group
to multiply? Are you happy with that?
Could you have done anything
different?

For Children, Too

What causes the most fights
between your brothers and sisters?

What is your favorite board game?

How much TV do you watch a week?
What is your favorite show?

❖

What makes you the angriest and
what do you do with your anger?

❖

What do you want to be when you
grow up?

❖

Do you earn your own money? If so,
what are you saving for?

❥

How do you talk to God?

❥

What is your favorite sport?

❥

Which chores around the house are
you responsible for?

What is your least favorite chore?

What is your favorite subject in school?

What is your worst subject in school?

If you could go anywhere in the world, where would you go?

What is your favorite toy?

What was your best vacation?

Have you ever told a lie, and did
you get caught?

What is your favorite pet?

Are you a morning person or a
night person?

❏

What is the greatest gift you have
ever received?

❏

What is the best gift you have
ever given?

❏

If somebody is teasing somebody at
school, do you join in, try to stop
it or ignore it?

ν

How do you feel about giving your
money to help others or to
the church?

ν

If you could be any cartoon character,
which one would you be and why?

ν

What is the most adventurous thing
you have ever done?

If you could ask God for anything,
what would it be?

What is the best birthday party
you ever had?

How do you feel when you get
home from school?

❖

If you found $20 on the street,
would you tell anybody?

❖

What do you like most about
church?

❖

If you could see one television star
get saved, who would it be?

∀

When your family is fighting, how
does it make you feel?

∀

If you could visit with an angel,
what would you ask him?

∀

Who had the most influence
on your decision to
receive Christ?

What About
Your Dreams?

What is the most fulfilling work you
have ever done?

If you could spend the rest of your
life doing exactly what you wanted,
what would you do?

What is the one thing you want to
accomplish next week?

A skill I would like to acquire is
_____. Why?

Share a dream you have that
has not come true ... yet.

If you could spend an afternoon with
anyone in the world, who would that
person be (besides God)?

❯

What is one of your goals in life?

❯

What is one thing you want to accomplish in the next five years?

❯

If you could go anywhere on a trip right now and money was no object, where would you go and why?

If you could do anything you wanted
to do, what would you do?

If you could wake up tomorrow
having gained only one quality or
ability, what would it be?

What is your greatest need for
the coming year?

If you had enough money to do anything you wanted, what would you do?

If you knew you could not fail, what would you do?

When you retire, what do you want to do?

What is your dream job?

Is there something you've dreamed
of doing for a long time?
Why haven't you done it?

Do you feel stuck in your life goals?
What are you doing to get out of
being stuck?

A Look at the Past
(great for when visitors are present)

❖

Where did you grow up?

❖

How many people were in your family?

Where have you traveled?

What are some of the
accomplishments in your life?

What was your family's view of God?

Tell us where you were born and
something you remember about the
place that your family lived when
you were very young.

∨

What are some great traditions in
your family?

∨

Which family traits have you
inherited that you like? Dislike?

∨

Which item that's been handed
down in your family do you have?

❦

Where did you go to school?

❦

What was your favorite subject in school?

❦

In what extra-curricular activities did you participate in school?

What was your first job?

What is the neatest thing you have
ever done?

What is the most courageous thing
you have ever done?

The Quaker Questions:
(To be used together)

- Where did you live between the ages of 7 and 12 and how many brothers and sisters did you have?

- What kind of transportation did your family use?

- Who was the person you felt closest to?

- When did God become more than a word to you?

What If . . .

If you were given a large amount of
money, what would you do first?

If you were in a circus, who would
you be?

You are at a friend's house for dinner
and you find a dead bug in your
salad. What do you do?

If you could choose the plot of the
dream you will have tonight,
what would it be?

If your house were on fire, which
three items (not people) would you
try to save?

∀

If you had a web site that described
who you are and what you are
about, what would it be like?
Describe it.

∀

If you were told that you must join a
military service, which branch would
you choose?

If you could be the manager/coach
of any professional sports
team, which would you choose?
Why?

If your family made a calendar, what
picture would you put for the
month of December?

If you were given a budget to produce a one-hour TV show, what would you do and with whom would you do it?

If you were stuck on a 12-hour flight to Korea, whom would you choose to sit next to you?
Why?

If a sex offender moved in next door
to you, would you move, witness,
protest or just pray?

If a meteorite were going to hit
the earth in one month, what
would you do next?

If you were shipwrecked on a deserted island, which one tool would you want to have with you?

If you had a time machine that would work only once, what point in the future or in the past would you visit?

⋎

If you could do anything and all of your bills were taken care of, what would you do?

⋎

If you had to give away one limb of your body, what would it be and why?

If you had to give away one thing
you owned, what would you give
and why?

If you have two tickets to the concert
of the lifetime and your best friend is
sick and needs you to take care of
her kids, what would you do?

If you were dying and you could
be with only one person, who
would it be?

If your life was a Wal-Mart store and
you could exchange one thing, what
would you exchange and why?

❯

If money were no object, what kind of party would you throw for your friends?

❯

If you could be any cartoon character, which one would you be and why?

Ten Icebreakers
<u>NEVER</u> TO USE!

NEVER USE THESE ICEBREAKERS!

What is the biggest stronghold in your life right now?

What is one secret you have never told your spouse?

Tell us about the time in your life when you felt like a great failure.

NEVER USE THESE ICEBREAKERS!

What event in King David's life can you relate to the most?
(Or any other Bible knowledge question that would alienate people.)

What is one thing you would like to change about the person to your right?

NEVER USE THESE ICEBREAKERS!

Y

What is the worst name you have ever been called?

Y

Turn to the person on your left and tell us how he or she could be a better parent.

Y

Name a sin of someone in the room so we can pray for that person.

NEVER USE THESE ICEBREAKERS!

∀

What gossip have you heard this week?

∀

What do you hate about our pastor?

Notes

Notes

_____

_____

_____

_____

_____

_____

_____

_____

_____

_____

Notes

_____

_____

_____

_____

_____

_____

_____

_____

_____

_____

Notes

_____

_____

_____

_____

_____

_____

_____

_____

_____

_____

Notes